THE HEROES PRINCIPLE

APPLYING VIRTUES THAT PRODUCE FAVOR

DR. ED TUROSE

THE HEROES PRINCIPLE

APPLYING VIRTUES THAT PRODUCE FAVOR

© 2015 Ed Turose.

Printed in the USA

ISBN (Print Version): 978-0-9903235-8-7

ISBN (Electronic Version): 978-0-9903235-9-4

This book has been prepared for publication by Wendy K. Walters and Palm Tree Publications, a division of Palm Tree Productions.
www.palmtreeproductions.com | www.wendykwalters.com

To Contact the Author:

EDTUROSE.COM

CONTENTS

5   **FOCUSIZE**

9   **SUPERHEROES**

13   **LACK OF LEADERSHIP**

25   **THE HEROES PRINCIPLE**

69   **FAVOR**

73   **PERSONAL EXAMPLES**

85   **40 DAYS OF FOCUS**

91   **SUMMARY**

95   **MEET DR. ED TUROSE**

Do not go where the

path may lead,

go instead where there is

no path and leave a trail.

–RALPH WALDO EMERSON

CHAPTER ONE

FOCUSIZE

I have a vision to train up a new breed of leaders. Many professional sports teams, when they are not achieving at a high level of success, go back to reviewing the basics. I believe these six principles have been lost in our society in recent years. Working in Fortune 500 companies for over 35 years, I am seeing a change in specific behaviors that are affecting the area of relationship building that affect the levels of success.

I want to help you focus on integrating these six powerful principles but we all know we live in a world full of distractions. A person who develops a lifestyle of focus can achieve higher and greater levels of success! The decisions you make to implement these principles after you read this book will dramatically affect your life and your future!

I call this "focusize" which is the exercising of your ability to focus every day. In order to get in physical shape, you need to exercise every day doing exercises to get your body in shape you want to portray. The same goes for exercising your thoughts and actions by staying focused.

Let's begin by defining the word focus.

- directed attention (attend – to apply one's self, to apply the mind)

- a point of concentration; to bring or direct toward a common objective

As mentioned earlier, when you begin to daily direct your attention and apply your mind towards a common objective, you are focusizing, or exercising your ability to focus. You must begin to understand that staying focused every day is critical to your success. Most people are easily distracted and end up not achieving their goals or objectives.

According to Webster's Dictionary distract is described as:

- to turn aside: divert

- to draw or direct (as one's attention) to a different object or in different directions at the same time

- to stir up or confuse with conflicting emotions or motives

Dr. Kevin Elko, leading sports psychologist, says, "In order to stay focused you have got to keep the main thing the main thing." You cannot allow distractions, disturbances, or disruptions to come in and take you away from your main objective where you are keeping your focus.

Success is described as a favorable or desired outcome, attainment of wealth, favor, or eminence. Most people get caught up in the distractions and end up maintaining a mundane or average lifestyle feeling frustrated when they do not meet their goals or objectives.

In consistency lies the power for success!

If we can stay consistent by developing specific processes in our life and stay focused on these processes, success will follow us! So let's begin with the process of implementing these six powerful principles that can reshape your life and meet your results.

A person who develops

a lifestyle of focus can

achieve higher and

greater levels of success!

2 CHAPTER TWO

SUPERHEROES

*Be more concerned with your character than
your reputation, because your character is
what you really are, while your reputation
is merely what others think you are.*

—JOHN WOODEN

A superhero is a fictional character that has amazing powers. We live in a world that has a fantasy with superheroes. It seems that heroes provide us with confidence in uncertain times. The numbers are bearing out that trust and confidence are at an all-time low in all areas of society.

In the late 1930s and early 1940s comic books introduced superheroes beginning with characters like Superman and Batman. During World War II, they became literal stars branching out into books, television shows, and action figures. The first Action Comics was published in 1938, which was Superman. Most of us spent hours watching the old black and white TV shows of Superman saving the day. In 1941, the first female, Wonder Woman, was introduced. In the 1960s and 1970s TV shows began to feature Batman, Robin, and such evil villains such as the Penguin, the Joker and the Riddler. Eventually, many sequels followed, and now they have become the top grossing films in Hollywood. (Source: *Mania*)

The top box office movies that are grossing the highest profits are the ones which have a hero or heroes attached to the storyline. The Avengers, Iron Man, Batman, Spider-Man, Superman, and Captain America all are on the top list and the top 10 super hero movies have grossed over $3.6 billion dollars. (Source: *Box Office Mojo*)

Jacqueline Thursby, Professor of folklore and English education, believes that part of the reason for superhero popularity is that Americans like imaginative entertainment. "They enjoy the suspension of belief and excitement hero figures in films offer," Thursby said. "We like to see variant presentations of familiar heroes. That is why we don't get bored. It is fun and refreshing to find variety in the familiar." Thursby also believes that superheroes restore hope.

"Everyone, at some time or another, needs to be rescued," Thursby said. "It might be rescued from illness, loneliness, too much work, etc., and hero figures provide temporary escape." It seems that these superheroes have become our role models since they always come out on top.

However, when we try to look up to people in today's society such as sports figures, artists, musicians, politicians, or business leaders, we see both moral and ethical failure.

Every one of us has been born with specific gifts, talents and abilities, however, we each need to learn how to develop, nurture and mature in these three areas. Most people do nothing with their gift, or are functioning at a very low level in their gift.

In addition, we need to gain acquired skills. When you understand your gifts and begin to develop acquired skills, you will see promotion, favor and success.

When you understand your gifts and begin to develop acquired skills, you will see promotion, favor and success.

3 CHAPTER THREE

LACK OF LEADERSHIP

*A startling 86 percent of respondents to the
Survey on the Global Agenda agree that we
have a leadership crisis in the world today.
Why would they say this? Perhaps because the
international community has largely failed to
address any major global issue in recent years.*

—SHIZA SHAHID

The definition of a leader is a person who rules or guides or inspires others. I have seen both good and bad leaders in the past 35 years in Fortune 500 companies. There have been many articles written about leaders and leadership. Here are a few thoughts on great leaders from my career experience. Leaders employ the following traits:

HANDS-ON

Leaders who are willing to roll up their sleeves and offer their expertise, support and encouragement to their team will see more productive results. I have had leaders who say, "I pay you to make the decisions" … and when you do not achieve the results all the blame goes on you. They never wanted to get involved and yet the outcome in most cases affected the entire team results. Leaders who are hands on, however, pull their weight to achieve the desired outcome. They motivate and move toward the goal.

A leader is one who knows the way,
goes the way, and shows the way.
—JOHN MAXWELL

Example is not the main thing in influencing
others, it is the only thing.
—ALBERT SCHWEITZER

UNITY

How can two walk together unless they agree? There is power in unity where one corporate voice, one vision, one unified body can make things happen and change the outcomes. Not only will the ride be smoother, but you usually arrive there more quickly when everyone is on the same page.

My opinion, my conviction, gains immensely
in strength and sureness the minute
a second mind has adopted it.
—NOVALIS

No one can whistle a symphony. It takes
an orchestra to play it together.
—H.E. LUCCICK

RELATIONSHIP

Many of us put many hours into our occupation and the family suffers. Those leaders that promote a family atmosphere will produce greater results. Great leaders know the people working for them as well as those in their personal lives—their spouse, children, family members. They implement specific things that are applicable to that family, making it more relational and creating a more productive environment.

When something is missing in your life,
it usually turns out to be someone.
—ROBERT BRAULT

Outstanding leaders go out of the the way to boost
the self-esteem of their personnel. If people believe in
themselves, it's amazing what they can accomplish.
—SAM WALTON

Become the kind of leader that people would follow
voluntarily; even if you had no title or position.
—BRIAN TRACY

ACCOUNTABILITY

Many individuals work independently and have never been challenged to submit to a higher authority to become accountable. Without accountability, there will be no order. The greatest successes I have encountered in my personal and professional life is when I was held accountable by someone greater than myself.

*A body of men holding themselves accountable
to nobody ought not to be trusted by anybody.*
—THOMAS PAINE

Accountability breeds response-ability.
—STEPHEN COVEY

*Accountability is the currency of success. Feedback
is the breakfast of champions—providing you
with both awareness and ideas for growth.
Accountability is fuel for reaching your potential.*
—WENDY K. WALTERS

RISK-TAKERS

Change is inevitable and is constant. Great leaders constantly look ahead and are willing to take a risk, even if it might end in failure. I recently heard a statement from a CEO of a large company that if his people do not make at least two mistakes per year then they are not doing their job effectively. The key is to learn from those mistakes and establish key learnings on an on-going basis. Key learnings are based on reviewing what has worked and what has not worked in a given time frame. Each area is then documented so you do not make the same mistakes again.

Only those who risk going too far can possibly find out how far one can go.

—T.S. ELIOT

You've got to go out on a limb sometimes because that's where the fruit is.

—WILL ROGERS

SENSITIVITY

People go through seasons of ups and downs and some are truly hurting. We need to be sensitive to people when they are going through these seasons since in most cases it has a tendency to affect their work productivity and results. For example, if a family is going through a divorce, a sickness, or loss of loved one, a manager needs to provide sympathy and understanding during these times.

Resolve to be tender with the young, compassionate with the aged, sympathetic with the striving, and tolerant of the weak and the wrong. Sometime in life you will have been all of these.

—LLOYD SHEARER

If we are to live together in peace, we must come to know each other better.

—LYNDON JOHNSON

OPEN TO NEW IDEAS

Great leaders allow all participants to share their ideas. Many times certain behavioral styles dominate and drive their own ideas and do not allow or forget to provide others the time to share in a group or personal setting. Nobody likes working for someone who thinks they know it all. Without an open forum to discuss and strategize new ideas, the environment of creativity gets stagnant.

Those who cannot change their minds cannot change anything.

—GEORGE BERNARD SHAW

Your assumptions are your windows on the world. Scrub them off every once in a while, or the light won't come in.

—ISAAC ASIMOV

OVER-COMMUNICATE

This is one of the most frustrating areas that I hear from people while working within an organization or team concept. Leaders that over communicate will keep their team members engaged, meet specific deadlines and help each team member understand the expectations of the project tasks. Weekly updates will keep your team focused on achieving the corporate and personal goals and objectives.

Precision of communication is important, more important than ever, in our era of hair trigger balances, when a false or misunderstood word may create as much disaster as a sudden thoughtless act.

—JAMES THURBER

You can have brilliant ideas, but if you can't get them across, your ideas won't get you anywhere.

—LEE IACOCCA

SUPPORTIVE

Everyone needs support from their leader when they are struggling to achieve their goals and objectives. As mentioned before, great leaders will offer their support along with bringing other team members or peers to provide additional encouragement and assistance. One way to be supportive of the entire team is to share successes within the team that might help support some other.

Each person on a team is an extension of your leadership; if they feel empowered by you they will magnify your power to lead. Trust is a great force multiplier.

—TOM RIDGE

A good leader accepts your past, supports your present, and encourages your future.

—UNKNOWN

ACTIVE LISTENER

With the busyness of this age of technology, we sometimes react verses responding to a situation and fail to listen for the most accurate information. Many times as my team shares with me the information they are receiving from our customers, I always make sure they go back and ask more questions to acquire the best, accurate information. In addition, I always make sure as a leader I am listening to my team members to maintain a positive working environment.

Most people do not listen with the intent to understand; they listen with the intent to reply.
—STEPHEN R. COVEY

Listening is a magnetic and strange thing, a creative force. Those who listen to us are the ones we move toward. When we are listened to, it creates us, makes us unfold and expand.
—KARL A. MENNINGER

TEN TRAITS OF A GOOD LEADER

1. They are hands-on.

2. They foster unity.

3. They value relationship.

4. They practice accountability.

5. They are risk-takers.

6. They operate with sensitivity to others.

7. They are open to new ideas.

8. They over-communicate so they are understood.

9. They are supportive.

10. They are active listeners.

4 CHAPTER FOUR

THE HEROES PRINCIPLE

A hero is defined, according to Webster's dictionary, as *an illustrious warrior, a person admired for their great achievements and noble qualities or one who shows great courage.*

Hebrews 11 is the faith chapter that lists many of the heroes of faith in the Bible. In addition, here is a list of Biblical Heroes that you can study to gain valuable information from their lives.

JESUS THE GREATEST EXAMPLE

Jesus was the proto-type when it comes to applying these powerful principles into action. As you study scriptures of the life of Jesus, begin to review all the examples of how He walked daily in these six core principles and virtues that ministered to so many people in His day and beyond. He then began to show His disciples how to walk in these virtues. As they did, these 12 men turned the world upside down.

THE HEROES OF THE FAITH
Source: *FaithHub*

1. **David**: A man after God's own heart. He was the most heralded king of the united Kingdom of Israel. His life represented break and renewal.

2. **Abraham:** The father of the nation of Israel was already 75 when God directed him out of the land of his people. When tested to sacrifice his son, Abraham's declaration was that "God will provide the sacrifice!" This response is a testament to the man whose absolute trust and pursuit of God was "faith accorded to him as righteousness."

3. **Nehemiah:** Upon learning that Jerusalem, the city of his forefathers and the location of the Temple of God, was in ruins, Nehemiah petitioned the King to rebuild the walls of the city – and was himself sent to oversee their construction. He returned to King Artaxerxes after twelve years, a testament of submission, courage and dedication.

4. **Daniel:** He was carried away from the land of Israel while still a boy, groomed to be an advisor in King Nebuchadnezzar's court, rejecting the food of the king to keep the Law of Moses, a commitment he would keep into adulthood, eventually landing him in a pit of lions for refusing to call the king a god. Interpreting dreams and visions, Daniel would be a service to all kingdoms, and beheld the promise of God's coming rule. The prophet Ezekiel describes him as a "pattern of righteousness."

5. **Esther:** Born in exile, raised by her cousin Mordecai, she was chosen by the king for her beauty to be a faithful queen. Esther remained a faithful woman of God, fasting and praying while still maintaining devotion and submission to her king husband. It was her courage and dignity that saved the Jews of Persia from genocide.

6. **Peter:** When Jesus asked His disciples who they thought He was, Peter was quick to answer "You are the Christ, Son of the Living God!" As the leader of Jesus's apostles, Peter by no means led a perfect life. Brave and confrontational, he spent his life proclaiming the Gospel and living in community with the early Church.

7. **Paul:** A devout Jew and adamant in the destruction of the young Christian community, Saul of Tarsus would become the chief author of the New Testament and one of the first international missionaries. Though shipwrecked, imprisoned and tortured repeatedly, escaping angry crowds in various locations – Paul notes that his greatest care is the "daily pressure of concern for all the churches." Paul was content in all circumstances while spreading the Good News of Jesus across the Roman Empire, and becoming a spiritual patriarch of his day.

8. **Stephen:** He was one of the seven men chosen and was given the title of deacon, which literally means "to wait on tables," and these seven were basically the first pressed into serving on a church committee. He was the first person to be martyred for his belief in Christ. During his stoning, he humbly and boldly proclaimed his vision of the risen Lord seated at the right hand of the Father.

9. **Thomas:** For all his fame as the one who doubted Jesus' resurrection, the Apostle Thomas was a man of extraordinary deeds of faith. Thomas is the first of the disciples to declare Christ's singular divinity, calling him "my Lord and my God!" Tradition holds that

Thomas planted seven churches in India, where these small Christian communities still exist today – and are known as the Saint Thomas Christians.

10. **John:** Sometimes called the "Beloved Disciple," He witnessed Jesus' first resurrection, the Transfiguration and Jesus' prayers in Gethsemane. Paul calls him a "pillar" of the church. John would write the Gospel that explicitly states a divine identity of Christ (the famous John 1:1) and the Bible's perhaps most famous verse: John 3:16.

11. **Dorcas:** A woman focused on building the Kingdom in her era. A model to her community who dedicated her craft to help the poor in her territory.

12. **Ruth:** Ruth was poor and a foreigner, but she listened to the advice of Naomi where courage and ingenuity triumph over misfortune. Ruth, a childless widow at the beginning of the story, became the great-grandmother of Israel's great king, David.

THE HEROES PRINCIPLE

I want to give you my HEROES Principle, which are specific character traits that I believe can change your life if you begin to apply these principles into your daily routine. These six virtues call upon us to do what is right and avoid what it wrong.

VIRTUE: an admirable quality or attribute.

Society in general has loss these valuable principles that need to be reestablished in our personal and professional life. If you can begin to focus on and incorporate these into your life, you will see great favor and success.

My acronym for the HEROES Principle is listed below.

        H   **HONOR**

        E   **EXCELLENCE**

        R   **RESPONSIBILITY**

        O   **ORDER**

        E   **EXPECTATION**

        S   **SERVANTHOOD**

HONOR

Honor is the highest degree of respect, mingled with awe, for the dignity and character of another person. Honor is a good reputation, good quality or character as judged by other people, and high moral standards of behavior.

> *Honor recognizes that God has a plan*
> *to bring someone in your life so you will be more*
> *in God today that when you met them.*
>
> **—DR. MARK KAUFFMAN**

One thing that is lacking in today's society is honor. If you would begin to honor others by giving them the respect based on who they are as a person and not what they do, you would see an increase in building positive relationships. Honor is how you treat others and especially those who are your elders and peers.

We live in a world full of dishonor to those in authority, and even dishonoring those with different personality styles or cultural backgrounds than ours. Many of us have been dishonored by someone, but if you stay focused on honoring individuals, you will see that this character trait will serve you well in all you do in your life.

No person was ever honored for what he received.
Honor has been the reward for what he gave.
—CALVIN COOLIDGE

EXAMPLE OF EXCELLENCE: KING DAVID

King David demonstrated a beautiful example of honor when he had an opportunity to vanquish himself against a leader who had caused him a great deal of trouble unjustly.

And he came to the sheepcotes by the way, where was a cave; and Saul went in to cover his feet: and David and his men remained in the sides of the cave.

And the men of David said unto him, "Behold the day of which the Lord said unto thee, 'Behold, I will deliver thine enemy into thine hand, that thou mayest do to him as it shall seem good unto thee.'"

Then David arose, and cut off the skirt of Saul's robe privily. And it came to pass afterward, that David's heart smote him, because he had cut off Saul's skirt.

And he said unto his men, "The Lord forbid that I should do this thing unto my master, the Lord's anointed, to stretch forth mine hand against him, seeing he is the anointed of the Lord. So David stayed his servants with these words, and suffered them not to rise against Saul."

But Saul rose up out of the cave, and went on his way.
David also arose afterward, and went out of the cave,
and cried after Saul, saying, "My lord the king."

And when Saul looked behind him, David stooped
with his face to the earth, and bowed himself.

And David said to Saul, "Wherefore hearest thou men's words,
saying, 'Behold, David seeketh thy hurt? Behold, this day
thine eyes have seen how that the Lord had delivered thee
to day into mine hand in the cave: and some bade me kill
thee: but mine eye spared thee; and I said, I will not put forth
mine hand against my lord; for he is the Lord's anointed.'"

—1 SAMUEL 24:3-10

And now, behold, I know well that thou shalt
surely be king, and that the kingdom of Israel
shall be established in thine hand.
—1 SAMUEL 24:20

King David honored the office and anointing on the life of King Saul, despite all the times Saul tried to kill David. In the midst of this life and death situation, honor overcame and God brought judgment out of this act of honor. Even Saul knew that this act of honor would result in David becoming King.

"The Lord therefore be judge, and judge between
me and thee, and see, and plead my cause,
and deliver me out of thine hand."

*And it came to pass, when David had made an
end of speaking these words unto Saul, that Saul
said, "Is this thy voice, my son David?"*

And Saul lifted up his voice, and wept.

*And he said to David, "Thou art more righteous than I: for
thou hast rewarded me good, whereas I have rewarded
thee evil. And thou hast shewed this day how that thou
hast dealt well with me: forasmuch as when the Lord had
delivered me into thine hand, thou killedst me not.*

*"For if a man find his enemy, will he let him go well
away? wherefore the Lord reward thee good for that
thou hast done unto me this day. And now, behold, I
know well that thou shalt surely be king, and that the
kingdom of Israel shall be established in thine hand."*

—1 SAMUEL 24:15-20

SCRIPTURES ON HONOR

The following are scriptures which focus on several different
areas of honor.

PROFESSIONAL HONOR FOCUS

*Honor everyone. Love the brotherhood.
Fear God. Honor the king.*

—1 PETER:17

SUBMISSION TO THOSE IN AUTHORITY

Let every person be subject to the governing authorities.
For there is no authority except from God, and those
that exist have been instituted by God. Therefore
whoever resists the authorities resists what God has
appointed, and those who resist will incur judgment.
—ROMANS 13:1-2

Render to all men their dues. [Pay] taxes to whom taxes
are due, revenue to whom revenue is due, respect to
whom respect is due, and honor to whom honor is due.
—ROMANS 13:7 AMP

Let us live and conduct ourselves honorably and
becomingly as in the [open light of] day.
—ROMANS 13:13A AMP

Servants, obey in all things your masters according
to the flesh; not with eyeservice, as menpleasers;
but in singleness of heart, fearing God;
—COLOSSIANS 3:22 KJV

Honor is the greatest seed you can sow!
—DR. MARK KAUFFMAN

EXAMPLES OF HOW TO USE HONOR IN THE WORKPLACE

Do you honor your position in your workplace? As a Christian, you have been given the authority to control the atmosphere in your work environment. As you bring honor in this arena, you will see strife, conflict and disunity leave but you must take the spiritual stand in the workplace. You must lead by example and become the light in a world full of darkness.

Do you honor your superiors and supervisor whom you report to? Do you respect their title and function? The greatest way to honor a peer or a superior in the workplace is to serve them. They have been given a specific title and function that needs to be honored such as President or Vice President as they are being introduced to others. Remember, according to Romans 13:1, God has placed the ones in authority over us and we must respect and honor that authority.

Do you honor the people you work with? Many people in the workplace are complainers, moaners, grumblers, faultfinders, backbiters and gossipers. What about you? You have got to be careful that you do not allow yourself to join in with these people who, in most cases, are just there to collect a paycheck. Passion in what you do rules! When you stay above the situation and keep a positive attitude, then favor and success will come your way. This will be a testimony for you to share of how honor brings promotion and success!

PERSONAL HONOR FOCUS

So then, whether you eat or drink, or whatever you
may do, do all for the honor and glory of God.
—1 CORINTHIANS 10:31 KJV

Love one another with brotherly affection [as members of one family], giving precedence and showing honor to one another.
—**ROMANS 12:10 AMP**

Honor (esteem and value as precious) your father and your mother—this is the first commandment with a promise—That all may be well with you and that you may live long on the earth.
—**EPHESIANS 6:2-3 AMP**

Honor the Lord with your capital and sufficiency [from righteous labors] and with the firstfruits of all your income;
—**PROVERBS 3:9 AMP**

Does everything you do honor and glorify God? If we do not know how to honor God, then how will we know how to honor our family, friends, associates or co-workers?

Do you honor your spouse? It is amazing how many spouses dishonor each other even in a kidding manner with their words. Do you still open the door for your wife, walk with her instead of in front of her, or allow her to go first in even ordering a meal? Your children will notice how you honor each other and it can be handed down to each generation producing a culture of honor.

Do you honor your children and make a big deal of their accomplishments? By speaking words of honor over your children, power is released to build in them confidence and self-worth. Most individuals who have not grown up in a culture of honor have low self-esteem. Make sure you minimize their weaknesses and honor their strengths.

Do you honor your mother and father? This comes with a great promise of long life. I realized as a teenager as I was rebelling how much I hurt my parents and said some things I regretted later in life. When I got out on my own, I began to realize how much support they gave and how good I had it in those days. I repented and made sure they knew how appreciative I was for their love for me.

Do you honor God with your tithes, offerings, alms and first fruits? There is great blessing in honoring God with our time, talent and treasure in life.

A few simple ways to start honoring others is by saying. "Yes sir (or ma'am)," or "No sir (or ma'am)," and by calling older people by Mr. or Mrs. If you begin to respect titles of people and honor and respect those titles such as President, Dean, Principle, Pastor, Manager, Priest, and others, you will see them begin to treat you differently as you honor them.

PRACTICAL APPLICATION

- Begin to develop an attitude of honoring someone close to you such as family, friends, loved ones or a boss or mentor.

- You can start by addressing people by their title or saying yes sir when asked a specific question. If you begin to honor others you will see how they will begin to honor you!

- Please list two situations (individuals) that you need to focus on and restore relationship. The rewards of walking in the spirit of honor are waiting to manifest in your life.

EXCELLENCE

Excellence is doing something very good and to the best of your ability. Excellence is a choice; you were not born with it. Excellence is a privilege of a lifetime. You need to wake up every day and decide to walk in excellence. To excel means to be first in rank, above average, beyond the norm. Excellence is pouring out and demonstrating your best with what you have.

The quality of a person's life is in direct proportion
to their commitment to excellence, regardless
of their chosen field of endeavor.
—VINCE LOMBARDI

EXAMPLE OF EXCELLENCE: DANIEL

Forasmuch as an excellent spirit, and knowledge, and understanding, interpreting of dreams, and shewing of hard sentences, and dissolving of doubts, were found in the same Daniel, whom the king named Belteshazzar: now let Daniel be called, and he will shew the interpretation.
—DANIEL 5:12

I have even heard of thee, that the spirit of the gods is in thee, and that light and understanding and excellent wisdom is found in thee.
—DANIEL 5:14

Then this Daniel was preferred above the presidents and princes, because an excellent spirit was in him; and the king thought to set him over the whole realm.
—DANIEL 6:3

Excellence is always Plan A, never Plan B. It is Plan A or Plan A!
—JIM SANDERBECK

Do people say they have heard of you like it states in Daniel 5:14? His reputation preceded him in his sphere of influence because he was operating in a spirit of excellence in everything he did! We have lost this virtue in our culture today! It is amazing how people just do enough to get by in their workplace and home life. In Daniel 6:3 he was preferred above. The word preferred means more desirable and more valuable that the rest! If you begin to assimilate the spirit of excellence in your daily routine you will receive the same rewards that Daniel walked in – promotion, influence and increase in all areas of life!

SCRIPTURES ON EXCELLENCE

The following are scriptures which focus on several different areas of excellence.

PROFESSIONAL EXCELLENCE FOCUS

And whatsoever ye do, do it heartily, as
to the Lord, and not unto men.
—COLOSSIANS 3:23

And this is my prayer: that your love may abound more
and more in knowledge and depth of insight, so that
you may be able to discern what is excellent and may
be pure and blameless until the day of Christ, filled
with the fruit of righteousness that comes through
Jesus Christ—to the glory and praise of God.
—PHILIPPIANS 1:9-11 NIV

Whatever your hand finds to do, do it with all your might,
for in the realm of the dead, where you are going, there is
neither working nor planning nor knowledge nor wisdom.
—ECCLESIASTES 9:10 NIV

EXAMPLES OF HOW TO USE EXCELLENCE
IN THE WORKPLACE

Do you accomplish tasks with excellence? We live in a get it done quickly society and usually the job is not done with a spirit of excellence. Daniel's spirit of excellence made him 10 times greater than anyone else in his time on earth! His mindset became an operation of excellence.

What does excellence bring? Daniel could not do anything unless it had excellence attached to it. Like Daniel, Joseph received the same results: excellence got them noticed; they received promotion, access to everything, put in charge of their countries, and were placed into a position to change their culture. Maybe that next promotion will be given to you if you walk in the spirit of excellence!

PERSONAL EXCELLENCE FOCUS

He that hath knowledge spareth his words: and a
man of understanding is of an excellent spirit.
—PROVERBS 17:27

O Lord our Lord, how excellent is thy name in all the earth!
—PSALM 8:9

According to Gary Inrig, he provides a biblical model of excellence in 7 unique areas.

1. **It has a different standard—God.** The character of God provides the point of comparison when it comes to determining excellence and setting this standard for excellence results in humility not pride.

2. **It has a different model—Christ.** To live with excellence is to live as He lived (1 John 2:6).

3. **It has a different goal—Christlikeness.** It strives to achieve God's purpose for man that is for every Christian "to be conformed into the image of His Son."

4. **It has a different focus—character.** A person's character gives meaning to all that he does.

5. **It has a different basis—revealed truth.** Christians possess an absolute and revealed value system found in the Scriptures.

6. **It has a different motive—God's glory.** Every Christian's motive should be to please God and walk worthy of Him by revealing His character in all areas of life.

7. **It has a different enablement—grace.** We rely on God's grace through the indwelling of His Spirit that enables us to pursue excellence. His Spirit enables us to do what we otherwise cannot do – glorify God.

When you walk in excellence, you take ownership and 100% responsibility for your gifts and abilities. Most people are average and just do a job to get it done, but those who are HEROES, will do every job with the best of their ability and make sure it meets and exceeds the expectation of the person in charge.

Excellence will not tolerate unbelief, failure, procrastination, average, laziness, or the easy way out. Excellence is going the extra mile to do a better job than anyone else can do.

The heart of excellence is passion. Passion inspires people with energy, encouragement, and a positive environment. Excellence is alive with vision. When you get around people of excellence, you want to do something, go somewhere, and accomplish something enormous.

Be a yardstick of quality. Some people aren't used to
an environment where excellence is expected.
—STEVE JOBS

EXAMPLE

Excellence is doing the little things nobody notices like picking up paper in a public bathroom floor, taking a grocery cart back into the grocery store, or taking care of your personal things. Teenagers, you have the same opportunity by keeping your room cleaned, cutting your grass, or helping around the house to make sure things look good when others come to visit your home.

PRACTICAL APPLICATION

- Take inventory of your personal conduct or behavior and identify the areas that you need to change.

- Ask some close friends to help you identify a specific area where can grow in the area of excellence. You might be surprised at what you hear.

- Look for ways to improve a situation everyday by adding excellence to the mix.

RESPONSIBILITY

Responsibility is the state of being the person who caused something to happen, it is a duty or task that you are required or expected to do, something that you should do because it is morally right, and being held accountable for your actions.

The greatest day in your life and mine is when we take total responsibility for our attitudes. That's the day we truly grow up.
—JOHN C. MAXWELL

EXAMPLE OF RESPONSIBILITY: APOSTLE PAUL

Our orders—backed up by the Master, Jesus—are to refuse to have anything to do with those among you who are lazy and refuse to work the way we taught you.

Don't permit them to freeload on the rest. We showed you how to pull your weight when we were with you, so get on with it. We didn't sit around on our hands expecting others to take care of us.

In fact, we worked our fingers to the bone, up half the night moonlighting so you wouldn't be burdened with taking care of us. And it wasn't because we didn't have a right to your support; we did.

We simply wanted to provide an example of diligence, hoping it would prove contagious.
—2 THESSALONIANS 3.6-9 MESSAGE

Don't you remember the rule we had when we lived with you? "If you don't work, you don't eat." And now we're getting reports that a bunch of lazy good-for-nothings are taking advantage of you. This must not be tolerated. We commanded them to get to work immediately—no excuses, no arguments—and earn their own keep. Friends, don't slack off in doing your duty.
—2 THESSALONIANS 3.10-13 MESSAGE

The Apostle Paul was very blunt in the above passage. If you do not work then you do not eat. There was a time in his ministry that he had to take up his occupational craft of tent making (Acts 18.3) and get provision. No entitlements in the Kingdom system! He commanded them to get to work and would not tolerate any excuses.

SCRIPTURES ON RESPONSIBILITY

The following are scriptures which focus on several different areas of responsibility.

PROFESSIONAL RESPONSIBILITY FOCUS

Pray in this way for kings and all others who are in authority over us, or are in places of high responsibility, so that we can live in peace and quietness, spending our time in godly living and thinking much about the Lord.
—1 TIMOTHY 2:2 TLB

And now, friends, we ask you to honor those leaders who work so hard for you, who have been given the responsibility of urging and guiding you along in your obedience. Overwhelm them with appreciation and love!
—1 THESSALONIANS 5:12-13 MESSAGE

EXAMPLES HOW TO USE RESPONSIBILITY
IN THE WORKPLACE

Don't Pass the Blame: It is amazing to me how many people, when they have done something wrong in the workplace, are so quick to blame someone else. Be honest; if you have the responsibility, then take it to the fullest extent and make things right.

Do You Pray for Those Who Have Responsibility Over You? I remember I was with the President of my division of a major corporation and I approached him and said I am making a commitment to pray for wisdom and insight for the leadership team. He acknowledged that prayer and within the next five years the innovation that came from my division had a success rate of new product launches over 90%! That is unheard of since most new items fail in the marketplace. In fact, these new items in my market did so well that I gained a leadership market share and continue to have that today. I believe my prayer (1 can put 1,000 to flight) affected this division of the company and is still the most profitable division to date.

PERSONAL RESPONSIBILITY FOCUS

Make a careful exploration of who you are and the work
you have been given, and then sink yourself into that.
Don't be impressed with yourself. Don't compare yourself

with others. Each of you must take responsibility for
doing the creative best you can with your own life.
—GALATIANS 6:5 MESSAGE

For the man who uses well what he is given shall
be given more, and he shall have abundance. But
from the man who is unfaithful, even what little
responsibility he has shall be taken from him.
—MATTHEW 25:29 TLB

"Much is required from those to whom much
is given, for their responsibility is greater.
—LUKE 12:48 TLB

Do you have an entitlement attitude or one of personal responsibility? According to Webster's Dictionary, entitlement is the feeling or belief that you deserve to be given something (such as special privileges). Compare that to the definition or responsibility which is the state of being the person who caused something to happen. What state of being do you operate in?

Unfaithful in a little, then unfaithful in much. Those individuals who take on personal responsibility for their actions, and are faithful in the little they have, will ultimately be rulers over much.

It is amazing to me the lack of personal responsibility that I have seen in recent years. Recently, a person decided to quit a job and instead of giving a two week's notice, they texted the employer and told them they were quitting and would not be in the office on Monday morning.

A local university professor told me recently how a President of a company that interviewed students from this university was appalled from the response he got from a student who interviewed with him. He said the student sent the President a text message back thanking him for the interview with text abbreviations and did not even think about sending him a written letter.

If you want to be a hero and succeed in life then start taking personal responsibility for your actions in your everyday walk. This means not to wait for something to come your way by chance or circumstance, but you take the initiative and respond to life's opportunities and challenges.

Don't let others make choices for you that you can make yourself. Take action and follow up so you can make great progress in achieving your goals in life. Look in the mirror because you are 100% responsible of where you are today and where you can go tomorrow. Choose well!

PRACTICAL APPLICATION

- Start taking responsibility in a small thing and then work your way up to greater areas of responsibility. If you are unfaithful in a small matter, then you will be unfaithful in a larger more important matter.

- When you start taking responsibility for your actions people will notice and then begin to ask you to take on greater responsibility which will provide you with greater rewards ahead. Be prepared for it!

- Identify an area where you need to step up and take more responsibility in and you will begin to see how others will compensate your actions.

ORDER

The word order means to arrange or organize in a logical or regular way, peaceful or well-behaved. Have you ever been in a place that lacks order or discipline? It can become chaotic and end up causing an atmosphere of strife. Nothing can harm a family, business or organization more than strife which is a bitter sometimes violent conflict or dissension. Strife causes friction, disunity, and conflict.

In order to gain greater productivity in any arena, you must prevent people from creating and maintaining an environment of strife. There are laws that govern our lives and keep society running effectively. Without law and order there would be chaos and it would be survival of the fittest and everyman for himself.

EXAMPLE OF ORDER: KING DAVID

And David went out whithersoever Saul sent him, and behaved himself wisely: and Saul set him over the men of war, and he was accepted in the sight of all the people, and also in the sight of Saul's servants.
—1 SAMUEL 18:5

And David behaved himself wisely in all his ways; and the Lord was with him. Wherefore when Saul saw that he behaved himself very wisely, he was afraid of him.
—1 SAMUEL 18:14-15

Then the princes of the Philistines went forth: and it came to pass, after they went forth, that David behaved himself more wisely than all the servants of Saul; so that his name was much set by.
—1 SAMUEL 18:30

David knew God had anointed him King, however, he behaved himself in an orderly manner. He understood the proper protocol that he was under during the reign of King Saul. David could have gotten out ahead of God and broke the current order and covering he was under, but he behaved himself more wisely than all the servants of Saul. Headship and covering are key elements to stay in proper order so that you are protected under your spiritual covering.

Behold, how good and how pleasant it is for
brethren to dwell together in unity!

It is like the precious ointment upon the head, that
ran down upon the beard, even Aaron's beard:
that went down to the skirts of his garments;

As the dew of Hermon, and as the dew that descended
upon the mountains of Zion: for there the Lord
commanded the blessing, even life for evermore.
—PSALMS 133

In Psalms 133, the direction of the anointing flows down. When you get out of order you will not see the results of Psalms 133 which is the blessing! Stay in proper order and stay under the covering of your set man or woman of God and receive the commanded blessing of the Lord.

SCRIPTURES ON ORDER

The following are scriptures which focus on several different areas regarding order.

PROFESSIONAL ORDER

Let all things be done decently and in order.
—1 CORINTHIANS 14:40

There is a protocol in the professional arena. I submit myself to the proper order of leadership. I do what they say and I do it to the best of my ability without complaining or grumbling.

As mentioned before, we have the authority to maintain a calm, productive environment without strife. We need to be the peacekeepers and peacemakers to drive the proper order in the workplace.

PERSONAL ORDER

Consider well the path of your feet, and let all your ways be established and ordered aright.
—PROVERBS 4:26

For yourselves know how ye ought to follow us: for we behaved not ourselves disorderly among you.
—2 THESSALONIANS 3:7

There must be order within your personal life which includes your spouse, your children, and your immediate family. The husband must take spiritual headship within the family and there must be a unity together of making decisions. How you raise your children and the time and energy you commit to them is critical in training up a culture filled with order.

There must be order in relationships outside the home which includes your religious and organizational ties. There is an order for those who lead and cover you within your church.

You must understand the proper government in the church and submit to that set man or woman that God has raised up over you. You must not backbite or criticize those who are over you because that is out of order and will cause division within a church or organization.

A hero will operate within the laws that are set before him or her. There are laws that are set in place in organizations. Working for Fortune 500 companies for most of my life, I had to obey the companies' Codes of Conduct policies and annually sign the policy document that I would conduct myself within their code. There were specific rules outlining the responsibilities, practices, ethical and moral codes that the organization expected me to operate from and conduct all my business affairs within.

PRACTICAL APPLICATION

- Is there anything in your life right now out of order? Please take personal inventory and identify a specific area that you can position back into an orderly area.

- Look for ways to change the atmosphere in your school, job or at home. If someone is operating in strife, then you offer harmony and peace.

EXPECTATION

Expectation is a belief and a strong hope that something will happen or is likely to happen. It is to anticipate or look forward to the coming or occurrence of something. Expectation is the mother of manifestation. We live in a world of a just get by attitude that says being "average" is okay. In fact, the news media is saying that young people today will not attain the financial status that their parents were able to achieve. I do not believe that news report, do you?

High expectations are the key to everything.
—SAM WALTON

Hope is favorable and confident expectation; it's an expectant attitude that something good is going to happen and things will work out, no matter what situation we're facing.
—JOYCE MEYER

The kind of expectation I am talking about is the hope identified in Hebrews 11.1. Now faith is the substance of things hoped for, the evidence of things not seen. The definition of Bible hope is not wishing or it might happen? No, it is an earnest expectation, it is like a chicken stretching its neck out going after a bug! It is aggressive and knows that it will come to pass. This is the type of expectation God wants us to walk in both professional and personally.

EXAMPLE OF EXPECTATION: JOSHUA

Only be thou strong and very courageous, that thou mayest observe to do according to all the law, which Moses my servant commanded thee: turn not from it [to] the right hand or [to] the left, that thou mayest prosper whithersoever thou goest.

This book of the law shall not depart out of thy mouth; but thou shalt meditate therein day and night, that thou mayest observe to do according to all that is written therein: for then thou shalt make thy way prosperous, and then thou shalt have good success.

Have not I commanded thee? Be strong and of a good courage; be not afraid, neither be thou dismayed: for the LORD thy God [is] with thee whithersoever thou goest.
—JOSHUA 1:7-9

There failed not ought of any good thing which the Lord had spoken unto the house of Israel; all came to pass.
—JOSHUA 21:45

And, behold, this day I am going the way of all the earth: and ye know in all your hearts and in all your souls, that not one thing hath failed of all the good things which the Lord your God spake concerning you; all are come to pass unto you, and not one thing hath failed thereof.
—JOSHUA 23:14

The expectation that Joshua had based on God's word to him and all of Israel once they crossed over to the Promised Land all proved out at the end. Everything that they had expected God to do He did! In Romans 4:19b, Abraham had to call those things which be not as though they were and he received his promise from God. The expectation of these great men of God produced the manifestation.

The woman with the issue of blood had an expectation that if she just touched the hem of Jesus' garment she would be healed! And she was made whole!

> *And a certain woman, which had an issue of blood twelve years, and had suffered many things of many physicians, and had spent all that she had, and was nothing bettered, but rather grew worse.*
>
> *When she had heard of Jesus, came in the press behind, and touched his garment.*
>
> *For she said, "If I may touch but his clothes, I shall be whole. And straightway the fountain of her blood was dried up; and she felt in her body that she was healed of that plague."*
> —MARK 5:25-29

I love the expectation of Mary, the mother of Jesus when she was visited by the angel. What expectation she had to believe God and the word from the angel.

*And Mary said, "Behold the handmaid of the Lord; be it unto
me according to thy word. And the angel departed from her."*
—LUKE 1:38

In the same spirit of faith, we need to lift up our expectation
to new levels and begin to decree and declare the promises of
God to be manifested in all areas of our lives – spirit, soul, body,
socially and financially.

SCRIPTURES ON EXPECTATION

The following are scriptures which focus on several different
areas concerning our expectation.

PROFESSIONAL EXPECTATION SCRIPTURES

*Now the God of hope fill you with all joy and
peace in believing, that ye may abound in hope,
through the power of the Holy Ghost.*
—ROMANS 15:13 KJV

*Let this same attitude and purpose and [humble]
mind be in you which was in Christ Jesus:
[Let Him be your example in humility.*
—PHILIPPIANS 2:5 AMP

When the economy goes down and recession hits, expectation
withers among more people. Based on behavioral styles, over
86% of the population is pessimistic. They do not expect any

good thing to happen to them. As a Christian, we need to be like Christ whose expectation was that when He laid hands on somebody or spoke the Word, they would be healed. In the same spirit of faith, God can use you in the workplace, but you need to be in the 14% who believe and have great expectation for a positive outcome and opportunities in every circumstance.

PERSONAL EXPECTATION SCRIPTURES

According to my earnest expectation and my hope,
that in nothing I shall be ashamed, but that with all
boldness, as always, so now also Christ shall be magnified
in my body, whether it be by life, or by death.
—**PHILIPPIANS 1:20 KJV**

Now unto him that is able to do exceeding
abundantly above all that we ask or think,
according to the power that worketh in us.
—**EPHESIANS 3:20 KJV**

For the earnest expectation of the creature waiteth
for the manifestation of the sons of God.
—**ROMANS 8:19 KJV**

This last scripture of Romans 8:19 is your key to success in life. Even creation has an earnest expectation that the sons of God (male/female) will be revealed. The Greek word is Strong's #G603 (apokaradokia) which means anxious and persistent expectation to watch with your head erect and outstretched for a manifestation. This is how our life must be lived on a daily basis.

We must have expectations in the promises of God and begin to confess and stand on His Word that they will be fulfilled. Our covenant is with Abraham (Genesis 12.2-3) that we have been empower to prosper and blessed to be a blessing! We must expect this to happen so we can bless others.

Expectation is greater than just wishing something is going to happen. In order to begin to expect things, you have got to see them before they happen; this is called faith! It is amazing to me that when Apple comes out with an announcement that they are launching a new product, the consumers have a great expectation that the new technology will meet their needs and wants. There is buzz everywhere and when you get your new iPhone everyone wants to see the new additions and usually it meets the expectation of the buyer.

In the same manner of anticipation, you need to raise your level of expectation that you will be an over achiever and reach the levels of success that will meet your needs and desires.

PRACTICAL APPLICATION

- Please review your current goals that you have set for yourself. Maybe you have not set any goals since only

3% of the population set goals? Setting goals is critical to your success.

- Identify opportunities that can help you achieve these goals. When you begin to study and invest in yourself to improve your skills, the investment will pay off in achieving your personal goals and desires.

- In a current situation that you are involved with, raise your expectation higher and add some type of action step to increase your expectation for greater results.

SERVANTHOOD

A servant is one who performs duties to serve others. To serve means to give the service and respect due to (a superior) and to comply with the commands or demands of someone or something.

There has been much talk about entitlement which means the feeling or belief that you deserve to be given something (such as special privileges). We have seen many individuals have an expectation to be served by the government, the upper class, big business, or some other source when the greatest satisfaction and approval comes from serving others.

*My fellow Americans, ask not what your country can
do for you, ask what you can do for your country.*
—JOHN F. KENNEDY

*Caring for persons, the more able and the less able serving
each other, is the rock upon which a good society is built.*
—ROBERT GREENLEAF

EXAMPLES OF SERVANTHOOD: JESUS

*A new commandment I give unto you, That ye love
one another; as I have loved you, that ye also love
one another. By this shall all men know that ye are
my disciples, if ye have love one to another.*
—JOHN 13:34

*The Spirit of the Lord is upon me, because he hath anointed
me to preach the gospel to the poor; he hath sent me to heal
the brokenhearted, to preach deliverance to the captives,
and recovering of sight to the blind, to set at liberty them
that are bruised, to preach the acceptable year of the Lord.*
—LUKE 4:18-19

In Luke 4, Jesus was anointed to serve those who were bound, broken, bruised, beaten and blind and to set them at liberty. We live in a world of hurting people without Jesus and since Christ is in us, we need to know we are anointed to do the same.

But he that is greatest among you shall be your servant.
—MATTHEW 23:11

SCRIPTURES ON SERVANTHOOD

The following are scriptures which focus on several different areas on servanthood.

PROFESSIONAL SERVANTHOOD SCRIPTURES

For we are his workmanship, created in Christ Jesus unto good works, which God hath before ordained that we should walk in them.
—EPHESIANS 2:10

If any man serve me, let him follow me; and where I am, there shall also my servant be: if any man serve me, him will [my] Father honour.
—JOHN 12:26

Not so shall it be among you; but whoever wishes to be great among you must be your servant.
—MATTHEW 20:26 AMP

PERSONAL SERVANTHOOD SCRIPTURES

As we have therefore opportunity, let us do good unto all men, especially unto them who are of the household of faith.
—GALATIANS 6:10

External [a]religious worship [[b]religion as it is expressed in outward acts] that is pure and unblemished in the sight

of God the Father is this: to visit and help and care for the
orphans and widows in their affliction and need, and to keep
oneself unspotted and uncontaminated from the world.
—JAMES 1:27 AMP

How do you serve others? Do you have favorites? If you have a peer or manager who has a different personality style than you do does that affect the way you serve them?

I have been known in my company as the one who serves. When my boss comes to town to work with me, I honor her and serve her by picking her up on time at the airport, providing her with an ice cold bottle of water and I introduce her as Vice President to people we meet and make sure she gets the respect and honor due her. I choose to serve her and others. Servanthood is a choice when we live in a society that is all "about me" with daily selfies and spending more time adding friends to our Facebook page than making ever-lasting relationship to serve others. If we can realize that even in the self-focused mindset, there are benefits when you serve others.

According to an article in *US News and World Report*, Mark Snyder, a psychologist and head of the Center for the Study of the Individual and Society at the University of Minnesota expresses that there are benefits to serving others especially in volunteerism. "People who volunteer to serve others tend to have higher self-esteem, psychological well-being, and happiness," Snyder says. "All of these things go up as their feelings of social connectedness goes up, which in reality, it does. It also improves their health and even their longevity."

Most people say they value volunteering to serve others because it's "the right thing to do," among other altruistic reasons. But the strongest drivers of successful volunteers are actually more self-focused, notes Allen Omoto, a professor of psychology at Claremont Graduate University in Claremont, Calif. There are five main reasons people volunteer, he says.

Three are "self-focused":

- **Understanding**: the desire to learn new things and acquire knowledge.

- **Esteem enhancement**: feeling better about yourself and finding greater stability in life.

- **Personal development**: acquiring new skills, testing your capabilities, and stretching yourself.

Two are "other-focused":

- **Sense of community**: making the world, or your piece of it, better.

- **Humanitarian values**: serving and helping others, often with a strong religious component

I want you to identify your current focused lifestyle of how you are serving others. I have pinpointed three areas where most individuals are currently living when it comes to their ability to stay focused and serve others in their lives. Which one are you living in?

SUFFICIENT FOCUS

Individuals focused on just enough to get by without trying to improve or better themselves. The focus is living a daily life of being adequate, sustainable and living in just enough for themselves with little or no motivation to go to a higher level of achievement. I have enough for me and mine and no more.

SELF-FOCUS

Individuals who are living for their own personal interest or advantage. The focus is self-seeking, involves ego and self-serving and they will do anything to get ahead.

SERVANT FOCUS

Individuals who are focused on helping others along with themselves to achieve their objectives and goals.

As an example, a friend of mine in Baltimore, MD, gives away a home every year. He invites young people from all over the U.S. to come to Baltimore and work for 2 weeks to refurbish a home and then they hand the keys over to the new owners. This volunteer event even has the mayor of the city attending and has affected the lives of hundreds of young people who are here to serve a deserving family.

PRACTICAL APPLICATION:

- Identify a place where you can improve your community or offer some type of humanitarian value.

- Look at ways to serve others on a daily basis such as helping an older person.

5 CHAPTER FIVE

FAVOR

*And I will make of you a great nation, and I will
bless you [with abundant increase of favors] and
make your name famous and distinguished, and
you will be a blessing [dispensing good to others].*

*And I will bless those who bless you [who
confer prosperity or happiness upon you]
and [a]curse him who curses or uses insolent
language toward you; in you will all the families
and kindred of the earth be blessed.*

—GENESIS 12:2-3 AMP

Our covenant as believers is the covenant of Abraham. We have been given an abundant increase of favor so that we are blessed to be a blessing on the earth! Jesus spoke to us in John 1 about the favor we would receive as His children.

For out of His fullness (abundance) we have all received [all had a share and we were all supplied with] one grace after another and spiritual blessing upon spiritual blessing and even favor upon favor and gift [heaped] upon gift.

—JOHN 1:16 AMP

When you begin to apply the HEROES Principle, you will begin to experience favor in your life. Favor is approval, support, popularity or preference to a person or group. Favor makes you irresistible and attracts others to you. Favor takes you to the top of your sphere and makes you look good. When you see favor comes into your life, you begin to draw others to you, to be like you, hang around you and follow you.

Favor puts you on the front line and helps you fulfill your destiny. It cannot be mediocre, ordinary or second rate. Favor is a powerful force that will bring important people to you. Favor will have people seek you out to invest in your dreams and ask how they can help you become even more successful.

However, if you do not invest in yourself, work on improving your strengths and practice these principles that you have learned in this book, you will be like the movie Groundhog Day, living the same average life over and over again with the same mundane results. It's time for you to fulfill your assignment and begin to influence your sphere with these powerful principles that will encourage others but also bring fulfillment to both your personal and professional life.

That ye be not slothful, but followers of them who through faith and patience inherit the promises.

—HEBREWS 6.12

Favor won't always come immediately. You have to put these principles in motion until it becomes a lifestyle. You will be tested and tried in these principles to see if your heart is true. Once you have shown yourself faithful, the Lord Himself will reward you and you will have become a new creation.

Favor puts you on the front line and helps you fulfill your destiny.

6

CHAPTER SIX

PERSONAL EXAMPLES

I want to relate a few personal stories of how the HEROES principle worked in the following examples. The first one involves me personally, the second one involves a relative of mine and the final example involves my pastor.

GOD REDEEMS ME

Then said he unto the disciples, it is
impossible but that offences will come.
—LUKE 17:1

After spending many years with a major Fortune 500 company and receiving very favorable performance recaps, I hit a major distraction. There was a severe accident involving my son and we had to personally take care of him as caregivers. During this time, this accident got me so focused on him that it affected all other areas of my life. I realized that he took preeminence, but I had to stay focused to maintain my job and my other family relationships.

The company I was working for had a grading system as follows:

- 5.0 – best of class – (very few received this performance rating)

- 4.0 – Above Standard – (some were able to attain this)

- 3.0 – Standard – you are doing your job effectively – (most received this grade)

- 2.0 – Below Standard

- 1.0 – It gets ugly!

Under a previous manager, I was averaging 3.0 and 4.0 ratings in all 5 of my key areas of focus. I got a new manager and his personality and mine were very different. Although his thinking processes were different from mine, he was one of the best managers I have seen in creating processes that produce great results. During a visit into my area in the fall of that year, he graded me very highly and we had a great work experience together. Six months later as I was in the company HQ receiving my final review for the previous year, he asked me what kind of year I had. I told him it was a great year compared to my peers, coming in second in volume achievement and number one in financial management which was a major focus area of the company.

My manager's response to me was that even though it was a good year for me, he did not like the way I got my results, so my performance rating became three 3.0's, and two 1.0's. I was now on 90 days probation and would be terminated after 90 days if I did not make some changes.

I was in shock since he had not worked with me for over six months and the last work together was favorable. What should I do? How should I respond? Was I going to honor or dishonor him? I personally know the Vice President of the company and I thought about calling him to complain. I could call Human Resources and complain. I could defend myself and show him to be in the wrong or I can shut up, remain focused and **honor** this man and let God redeem me.

But no weapon that is formed against you shall prosper, and every tongue <u>that shall rise against you in judgment you shall show to be in the wrong</u>.

This [peace, righteousness, security, triumph over opposition] is the heritage of the servants of the Lord [those in whom the ideal Servant of the Lord is reproduced]; this is the righteousness or the vindication which they obtain from Me [this is that which I impart to them as their justification], says the Lord.

—ISAIAH 54:17 AMP

I kept hearing that small still voice saying, "Let me defend you." I got counsel and decided not to defend myself to upper management and get focused! I began to stand on Isaiah 54:17 every day and began to raise my *expectation* up that God would redeem me!

I had to get to work spiritually by standing on God's word and naturally by WORKING on my assignments. I had to take personal *responsibility* and for the next 90 days, I refocused on my processes and areas where I might need to improve on. I had to provide weekly updates and follow through in areas that he felt I needed to change and improve in the areas that I was graded low on for the yearly performance evaluation. Every recap I put together and turned in, I did so with *excellence*.

A former peer of mine was promoted and given the task to hold me accountable on making the necessary changes. He flat out told me that I would be terminated in the 90 days, but he was there to see what I was doing to report back to my manager. One of the greatest areas where you can improve your focus is accountability. I stayed in **order** and did not call anybody to defend and complain. I kept focused with **expectation** that God would redeem me.

After working with me for six weeks, his conclusion was I just needed a few tweaks in only one area and reported back to my manager to change both 1.0 ratings back to 3.0. I worked hard for those 90 days and in the end I knew if I stayed focused, I would see a great result. I **served** both my peer who was working with me and also my manager. I wanted them to know I was committed to the success of the company, and that I was willing and knew how to make the necessary changes.

After 90 days I was in **expectation** that I made the necessary changes, **honored** the people over me, did my work with **excellence** and took personal **responsibility**. I knew what I was going to hear next –a "great job" from my manager. As I moved on to finish that year in managing my team, I did not take an offence or hold a grudge toward my manager. I saw his gifting and strengths and began to serve his vision for the region. Consequently, I also began to see my results improve to levels I never saw before. You see, I was walking in these six powerful principles and I was experiencing greater results in my personal and professional life.

The following March I was in the National Sales Meeting in Las Vegas when they announced the Sales Manager of the Year award winner for the prior year. That's right, my name was called and I was honored, along with my food broker, as the Manager and Broker of the Year! How could that be when I was on probation for 3 months? I became a Hero – I operated in all 6 of those powerful principles and God redeemed me!

I needed wisdom to stay focused until a certain reward become evident in front of my own eyes. Since that time, this manager has moved on and he plays a vital leadership role in that company and to this day we have a great relationship. He had a way of getting things done differently, and I needed to focus my execution on his way of doing things. By doing so, I got a great reward – standing on a platform in front of hundreds of my peers as the Sales Manager of the Year!

STAY THE COURSE – DON'T QUIT

My second story involves a relative of mine who was hired by a local marketing firm. After about six months, the President, who I knew personally, came to me and told me he had to let my relative go and was going to fire him. I asked him on what grounds would you fire this young man since I knew him all his life and saw great potential. He came up with many reasons for his dismissal that did not add up.

His first reason was that my relative did not know to write and formalize an email. I asked the President if someone ever sat down and showed him how to top line and bullet point an email response; he responded no. Secondly, he told me that he was not getting along with his boss, a woman who had a very controlling personality. I told him that no one in his office gets along with her and the rumors were that many people were going to quit if she didn't start managing their business more effectively and personally with her marketing reps.

I told him that this young man has a great work ethic. He laughed and said that he did not think so. He told me that he does not stay past 5:15 PM in the office. I asked him what the hours of operation were and he said 8:00 AM to 5:00 PM. He said he expected this young man to stay until he left which was around 7 PM. I asked him if he ever told the young man that and he responded no. He said that he should know better.

I stepped into this situation and asked the young man's father what he should do. He told me his advice to his son was to quit and move on. I told him that if he focused and made a few changes he would be able to save his job and gain the valuable experience he needed to further his career path. If this young man quit this job without making an effort to change and get focused, it would affect him in every job he took in the future. His father told me to take over and I coached this young man in the email writing, in blending his personality with his boss and making sure he checked with the President each day before he left the building if he needed him to do anything. I told him to **honor** the people God had placed over him and to make these changes and with **excellence**.

I brought all the family members together and began to pray for God to change this situation and turn it around. I told my relative that he needed to take personal **responsibility** for his future as we coached and guided him along the way. However, he needed to stay in **order**, keep his mouth shut and go do his work and let God redeem him. Many people did not like his boss and were just leaving the company and badmouthing everybody involved and I told him to stay in proper **order**.

After we prayed, I told him to watch God move. He began to stand on certain scriptures and began to lift up his **expectation** and know that he had a calling in the marketplace. This was just a test for him to overcome. He knew what he was learning in this company was preparing him for something bigger in a few years down the road. Don't blow your future by quitting when God will redeem you and is in the process of giving you an awesome testimony.

As he began to focus on these things and **served** both his immediate manger and the owner, his status in the organization began to change. Within two weeks he was moved under a different manager, who was more personable, and she began to mentor him. After a few months his former boss was terminated.

Within six months he was promoted over the entire central and western business units and became one of the top marketing sales representatives. During the next 18 months, he was the first marketing rep they promoted within the organization and moved to California from the East.

After five years with the company, he was recognized as one of the top producers, loves the Californian lifestyle, owns five surfboards and is loving life. He eventually left that position for a National Sales Management role with another company, oversees the entire country in sales and marketing because he had the experience from this past job that opened the door to a greater future. Why? He got focused and implemented the six powerful principles that promoted him to a greater level of success.

KEYS TO PROMOTION AND OWNERSHIP

My final example is about my Pastor who began working at a local floral shop when he was a teenager. The owner asked him if he had a desire to work in the back part of the store and learn how to design arrangements, which he agreed to try his hand in that part of the business. He took personal *responsibility* and began to develop his gift. Soon after, he began to get noticed for the **excellent** arrangements that were showing up around town.

Eventually, he was called in by the other local florist who owned the second oldest flower shop in America. The multiple owners offered him a position and the Lord told him to **honor** and **serve** the partners and especially the owner.

As the years went by most of the other partners passed away and the last one living was the primary owner. He asked my Pastor if he wanted to buy the shop since none of his children wanted to keep it going and he responded that he did not have the finances to buy the shop. The owner told him that he would give my Pastor a sum of money every year and that he would give that sum back to him (the owner) and he would one day own the second oldest flower shop in America. In essence he was getting the flower shop for free because he was operating in the HEROES Principles.

In the midst of this transition, the owner began to display some emotions that could have forced my Pastor to leave, but he continued to **honor**, **serve**, and operate in an **orderly** fashion with a spirit of **excellence** during the final years of the owner's life.

After the owner passed away, my Pastor went to the safe in the store and there was an insurance policy that paid off the debt of the floral shop to the owner's family, and my Pastor became the owner of the second oldest flower shop in America. His *expectation* was that God had this in His plan all along and this position within the community provides him with influence and stature.

The store has branched out as both flowers and giftware and is prospering within the community. Recently, the floral shop in which he first started working, which was in operation over 85 years, just closed their floral department and all the business went to my Pastor's flower shop, doubling his annual revenue. What a success story of utilizing the HEROES Principles that enabled my Pastor to be given the second oldest flower shop, elevating his sales into the top 100 flower shops in America.

<u>The HEROES Principle</u>
Honor
Excellence
Responsibility
Order
Expectation
Servanthood

Walking in these qualities will

bring you favor and blessing.

You will have better results and

experience increased success.

7

40 DAYS OF FOCUS

I want to challenge you to do a personal inventory of life. In these six areas, which ones do you feel confident that you already operate in? If so, ask some close friends, peers, or accountability partner if they feel the same way you do about a specific area.

What areas do you need to improve in? At the end of each of these six areas in the practical application section, you were asked to identify specific areas that you needed to work on to improve. I would suggest you take the next 40 days and begin to focus on one of these areas that you feel you need to improve on. You can make the change if you stay focused!

Let's begin to "FOCUSIZE" on the virtue that you feel has the greatest opportunity to improve within your life. By focusing on "one" of these every 40 days, you can begin to master all six areas within one year. Imagine the fruit of our labor that within one year great favor and blessing can begin to flow into your personal and professional life.

Here is an example of how you can take one area and focus on it for the next 40 days.

FOCUSIZE EXAMPLE:

40 Days of Focus   **Beginning Date:_____**

Area of Focus: HONOR

- **People or Task Focus Area:** Family members, peers, co-workers, or specific tasks.

- **Action Plan:** List specific areas you can focus on to make this change.

- **Weekly Recap:** List specific things you did during the day or week that made changes in your behavior.

FOCUSIZE EXAMPLE:

40 Days of Focus **Beginning Date:**_____

Area of Focus: EXCELLENCE

- **People or Task Focus Area:**

  - **Professional:** Improve my work by providing my manager with more detailed information and finish my work on time.

  - **Personal:** Improve the appearance of the inside and the curb appeal of my house.

- **Action Plan:**

  - **Professional:** Begin to over communicate with my manager so I know deadlines and the expectations of my tasks.

  - **Personal:** Develop a weekly cleaning schedule to improve the appearance of my home.

- **Weekly Recap:**

  - **Week One:** Was able to turn in my project to my manager with two days to spare and cleaned the outside of my home by raking leaves, cutting grass and doing trim.

You can take the example listed previously and add six more weeks to the process to take you to 40 days of focus.

FOCUSIZE EXAMPLE:

It is now your turn to create a 40 days of focus process based on your greatest opportunity area within the six HEROES Principles. I would encourage you to document your 40 days of focus in a personal journal so as you can review the improvement in each of the six principles.

40 Days of Focus   **Beginning Date:**_____

Area of Focus: _____

- **People or Task Focus Area:**

  - **Professional:**

  - **Personal:**

- **Action Plan:**

  - **Professional:**

  - **Personal:**

- **Weekly Recap:**

  - **Week One:**

Continue this process for all the remaining weeks that total your 40 Days of Focus. I recommend you keep a journal of your successes and take note of your key learnings on each virtue throughout the 40 day process.

We are what we

repeatedly do.

Excellence then,

is not an act,

but a habit.

—ARISTOTLE

8

CHAPTER EIGHT

SUMMARY

The opportunity to walk in these six powerful principles and virtues is now up to you. Each one of these areas can be applied by one key factor—YOUR choice. You choose to honor, serve and do everything in the spirit of excellence. You choose to take personal responsibility, walk in an orderly manner and live in a realm of expectation.

The HEROES Principles have been proven out through history in the lives of our Lord, Jesus Christ, the Apostles and many other great men and women in the Bible. Begin to read the scriptures again with a focus on these six principles. You will see how those who operated in these virtues were positively affected as they made the choice to function in these on a daily basis.

Your life will drastically change when you begin to operate in these practices. Before long you they will become second nature to you. You won't even have to think twice about how you will respond when opportunities arise that involve these six principles, you will just do the right thing.

However, you will begin to notice those who do not operate in these principles. It will be so clear to you that you are going to have to share your personal testimony about how these virtues changed your life and can affect others in the same powerful and positive way.

The HEROES Principles take you to a higher realm of living. Most people in the world do not operate in these areas and literally do the opposite. You have been equipped and trained as a hero, so go become a hero to someone else and train them to go to a higher level to enjoy life at its fullness.

Be careful for nothing; but in everything by prayer and supplication with thanksgiving let your requests be made known unto God.

And the peace of God, which passeth all understanding, shall keep your hearts and minds through Christ Jesus.

Finally, brethren, whatsoever things are true, whatsoever things are honest, whatsoever

*things are just, whatsoever things are pure,
whatsoever things are lovely, whatsoever things
are of good report; if there be any virtue, and
if there be any praise, think on these things.*

*Those things, which ye have both learned,
and received, and heard, and seen in me, do:
and the God of peace shall be with you.*
—Philippians 4.6-9

The HEROES principle

will take you to a

higher realm of living.

MEET THE AUTHOR

DR. ED TUROSE

U tilizing the gifting of exhortation and empowerment, Dr. Ed Turose bridges the gap between the marketplace, education, and ministry. His heart is to see individuals be equipped, trained, and mentored to impact and influence the seven mountains of society to build the Kingdom of God.

Dr. Ed Turose has more than 35 years of business experience as a people manager, trainer, and strategic planner for two Fortune 500 Companies: Uni-Lever and the Coca-Cola Company. He has also received his Doctorate of Divinity from Tabernacle Bible School and University.

His expertise involves marketing, training, consulting and strategic planning. He serves corporate and business clients as well as education, government, and nonprofit clients by offering strategic solutions that will increase profitability, productivity and efficiency.

Dr. Turose is the Focus Coach and has created **THE FOCUS SYSTEM** which helps people achieve better and greater results in their life. This system includes:

- *The Focused Fulfilled Life*—Book and Workbook.

- *Focused Insights*—preparing individuals with practical application in communication, collaboration, confidence, conflict resolution, creativity and character.

- *Focused Vision*—preparing individuals to achieve their vision in 6 key areas: passion, placement, plan, purpose, possibilities and peak performance.

To learn more, connect, or invite Ed to speak at your event visit:

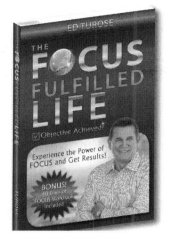

THE FOCUS FULFILLED LIFE

What would life be like if you could stay focused on a goal or objective and see greater results? People are consumed by an obsession to produce. This causes stress, anxiety, pressure and oppression. God's plan allows for a natural rhythm of work and rest that is overflowing with faith and hope, free from stress, filled with provision and designed for victory. In this book, *The Focus Fulfilled Life,* Ed shows you how to create a process for a lifestyle of focus by using the Word of God and activating your faith. A life of focus will produce a harvest of greater results. Experience the power of The Focus Fulfilled Life as you stand in faith and see a manifestation of the promises of God.

Your journey to see greater results begins with the Focus Fulfilled Life Progression!

- Identify Goals in your Spiritual, Emotional, Physical, Social and Financial Life

- Gather and Meditate on Specific Scriptures related to these Goals

- Develop Daily Strategies and Capture your Results

- Celebrate, Rest and Testify of God's Goodness and Faithfulness!

Available at EDTUROSE.com

FOCUSED DEVELOPMENT TOOLS
FOCUSED INSIGHTS

Focused Insights was created to help you gain an understanding of your personal identity and offer solutions to practically apply these solutions in your daily life. This knowledge and understanding of self will help you be able to process information and develop your soft skills.

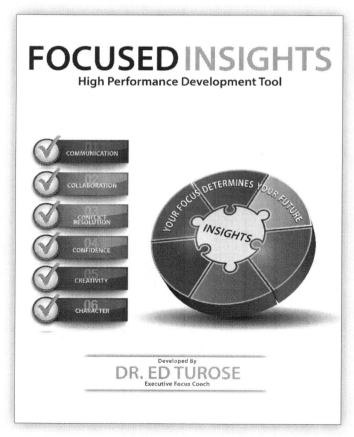

Available at EDTUROSE.com

FOCUSED DEVELOPMENT TOOLS
FOCUSED VISION

This program was created to help you make the best quality decision about your future. THE FOCUSED VISION HIGH PERFORMANCE DEVELOPMENT TOOL is one of the best resources available to get focused and waste no more time in gaining a complete understanding of your passion, your placement (sphere of influence) and what career is right for you. Get on the path to achieve your personal dreams and objectives today!

Available at EDTUROSE.com

FOCUSED DEVELOPMENT TOOLS
FOCUSED INSIGHTS

The Focused Interviewing for Job Placement Tool was designed to help you learn how to interview effectively to market your strengths to employers.

This three part series includes:

1. Platforms for Success

2. Career Development with The Focus Coach

3. Interviewing for Success

Plus Bonus CD-ROM: Interviewing for Success Workbook!

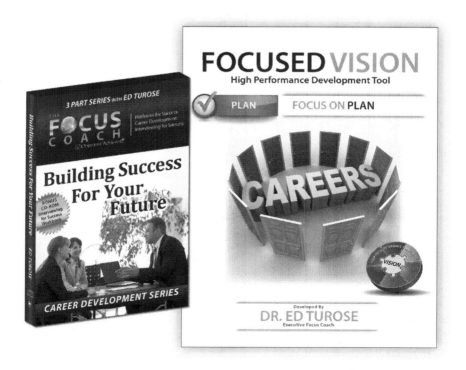

Available at EDTUROSE.com

Made in the USA
Columbia, SC
16 April 2018